Hailstones On Your Father

LEONARD BARRAS

An Iron Press Publication

First published 1979 by IRON Press
5 Marden Terrace, Cullercoats, North
Shields, Tyne & Wear NE30 4PD, UK.

Printed by Tyneside Free Press Workshop,
5 Charlotte Square, Newcastle-on-Tyne.

Front cover illustration by Carole Senior.
Book design and paste-up by Pete Swan.

ISBN – 0-906228-04-2.

IRON Press gratefully acknowledges the
financial assistance of Northern Arts.

Contents

The Artists' Names Are in Brackets.

SISTER MINNIE'S PEWTER PLANTPOT

Sister Minnie's pewter plantpot was a thing that she adored
  And it stood for many years on the shelf of the old dresser.
The plantpot was a present from Aunt Sal and Uncle Claude;
  They bought it on that self-same day that she was born, God bless her!
    And the midwife who delivered
    Took one look and stood and quivered.
    'A more repulsive thing you've never had'
    She told my dad.
And my mam broke down and cried; she felt a ninny.
      A more revolting thing they'd never had:
Not the plantpot – sister Minnie.

But she loved that pewter plantpot every single living day
  And believe me or believe me not it clattered off the shelf
On the very day that sister Minnie sadly passed away.
  Mind you, the two events, or so I've often told myself,
    Were not quite unconnected,
    For it's rather been suspected
      That when it fell it bumped her on the head
      And now she's dead.
Oh, sister Minnie's pewter plantpot – how she loved it!
      But when it fell it thumped her on the head.
The question was: Who shoved it?

PACE WILLIAM WORDSWORTH

Among untrodden ways I go,
  Where cattle safely browse,
Till butchers sally forth and O! –
  The difference to cows!

Behold that sheep upon the hill:
  He skips and lightly hops;
But soon he's on your butcher's bill
  As leg of lamb and chops.

We let the butcher wield the knife;
  We dodge those gentle eyes –
While each of us sustains his life
  With juicy steaks and pies.

NEUROTICS CHORUS

Whenever I'm happy I call to mind
That misery's not hard to find.
  There's a world out there
  That's full of despair,
So I scream a little scream:
  A-a-a-h!

Whenever I meet those cheerful chaps
Who smile and smile through all mishaps,
  Well, I just don't care.
  I've got my despair
And I scream a little scream:
  A-a-a-h!

  We can't always be depressed
  But we can do our best;
  If you can have a nightmare, why settle for a dream?
  Scream!

And the great religions have always taught
That life's inevitably fraught,
  So tear out your hair,
  Enjoy some despair
  (Some lovely despair)
  And scream a little scream:
A-a-a-a-a-h!

AVER

WAVE YOUR SONG SHEET

She's a fraulein from Borussia Monchengladbach
Just a fraulein from Borussia Monchengladbach.
How I would love her if I hadn't this bad back –
 Oh, this bad back!
There are lots of huge frauleins around in Bavaria,
But she's broader and taller and stronger and hairier:
 None could be grosser,
 Oh, no, sir,
 Than Rosa,
My fraulein from Borussia Monchengladbach!

NEITHER DO I

How often in the sad mid-afternoon
I've leapt up sleepless from the kitchen floor
And asked myself, how soon, how soon,
We'll meet again, or if we will, and if your leg still hurts.
How often in the sad mid-afternoon –
That time of day when ennui lays its blight –
I've called to mind that grievous night
I saw you last, and lost my braces at your Uncle Bert's.
Such strange concatenations
Provoked those odd enigmas!
You lost your combinations
(acquiring nasty stigmas).
To offer explanations
Would be to yeild up to the prurient world salacious titillations.
I much prefer to hug my self-respect
And I expect
You're similarly circumspect;
But oh! my dear,
Such pride, I fear,
Afflicts me sore
On the kitchen floor,
When I'm feeling bad
In the sad
Mid-afternoon.

FOLKLORE

Never hit your granny with a tankard of best bitter;
   The woman's not as bad as you might think.
So if the urge comes on you that makes you want to hit her,
   Use lemonade, for that's a softer drink.

BALD–HEADED LOVE SONG

Oh, I dream of a broken-down place in the hills
  Every night when the rain starts to pour,
    Where the wind always whistles
    Through bracken and thistles:
    That's the spot on the map
    Where a bald-headed chap
Is waiting for me by the door.

Oh, we're both of us not quite as young as we were;
  That's because we've grown older I think.
    Though with each year that passes
    I need stronger glasses
    And his teeth have dropped out
    Still that bald-headed lout
Is waiting for me by the sink.

And then at the last, when he's whispered goodbye
  And we've both of us turned ninety-seven,
    In a little while I'll
    Follow on with a smile,
    For I know there's a God
    And that bald-headed sod
Will be waiting for me up in heaven.

CONSTABLE'S CODE

When I was young, my sergeant said,
While wisely nodding his old head:
'Do nothing lad, that's bad or mean
And always keep your whistle clean'.

Well, through the years I've seen some sights,
Some nasty days and awkward nights
From Plymouth Hoe to Aberdeen,
But always kept my whistle clean.

Oh yes, I've kept my whistle clean
And what a dull old life it's been!
I hope some day I might be lucky –
And then I'll get my whistle mucky.

MOTHER NATURE'S BLOOMERS

See Mother Nature's bloomers here! –
  A pretty hopeless crew , sir.......
Who are this mob? I greatly fear
  They're you, madame, and you, sir!

You'd think the dear old girl would see
  It's time to stop and wonder
For mortal man's turned out to be
  Her most appalling blunder.

Mother nature's bloomers
Mother nature's bloomers
Mother nature's bloomers
  They're you, madame, and you, sir!

In time no doubt she'll glumly say
  'This lot could not be wetter'.
She'll scrap us all and start next day
  With something rather better.

But till at last she tries her luck
  With peewits pike or pumas,
The world is stuck – the world is stuck!
  With Mother Nature's bloomers.

Mother
Bloomers

THE GAS BOARD ARIA

Moonlight over the Gas Board office
  Shine kindly down on my sweet Billy.
When he clocks out from work this evening,
  Please rush him homeward willy-nilly.

He left my arms at eight this morning
  And I've been faithful, very nearly.
Moonlight over the Gas Board office,
  I love my Jack (I mean Bill) dearly.

Just lead him home – oh please remember!
  Bring him swiftly – back to my bed.
We might get married next September
  And he's not much good to me dead.

Deliver him to my embraces
  He isn't bright (you might say silly),
But moonlight over the Gas Board office,
  I'm all he's got – sweet simple Billy.

sweet billy

RAIN ON YOUR NEICE

I can't forget that night in June
   You said you loved another:
We parted at your garden gate
   And snow fell on your mother.

You whispered that I'd shared your love
   With up to half a dozen;
A teardrop glistened in your eye
   And wind blew round your cousin.

Your sister Lil, your Uncle Bill,
   And Auntie Jane dripped in the rain,
While Sam your dog howled through the fog.
   Was no-one spared that night of pain?

Oh, shall we ever love again?
   Perhaps I wouldn't rather
When I recall that night in June
   And hailstones on your father.

ARRIERE PENSEE

If Cleopatra's nose had just been shorter,
  The face of all the world would then have changed:
And as for me, I'd be no lamb for slaughter;
  My sorry life would quite be re-arranged.

For instance, I'd be blessed with God-like features.
  I'd love some gorgeous women, not in vain.
And my philosophy would better Nietzsche's:
  I'd have the sense to come in from the rain.

I'd have no dandruff or astigmatism.
  With Boycott, I'd be England's leading bat.
My brain would not be constantly in schism.
  I'd walk the earth and never fall down flat.

Well, Pascal's dictum seems a pretty strong one,
  But what does it avail us in the end?
For Cleopatra's nose remained a long one,
  And I'm a useless sod without a friend.

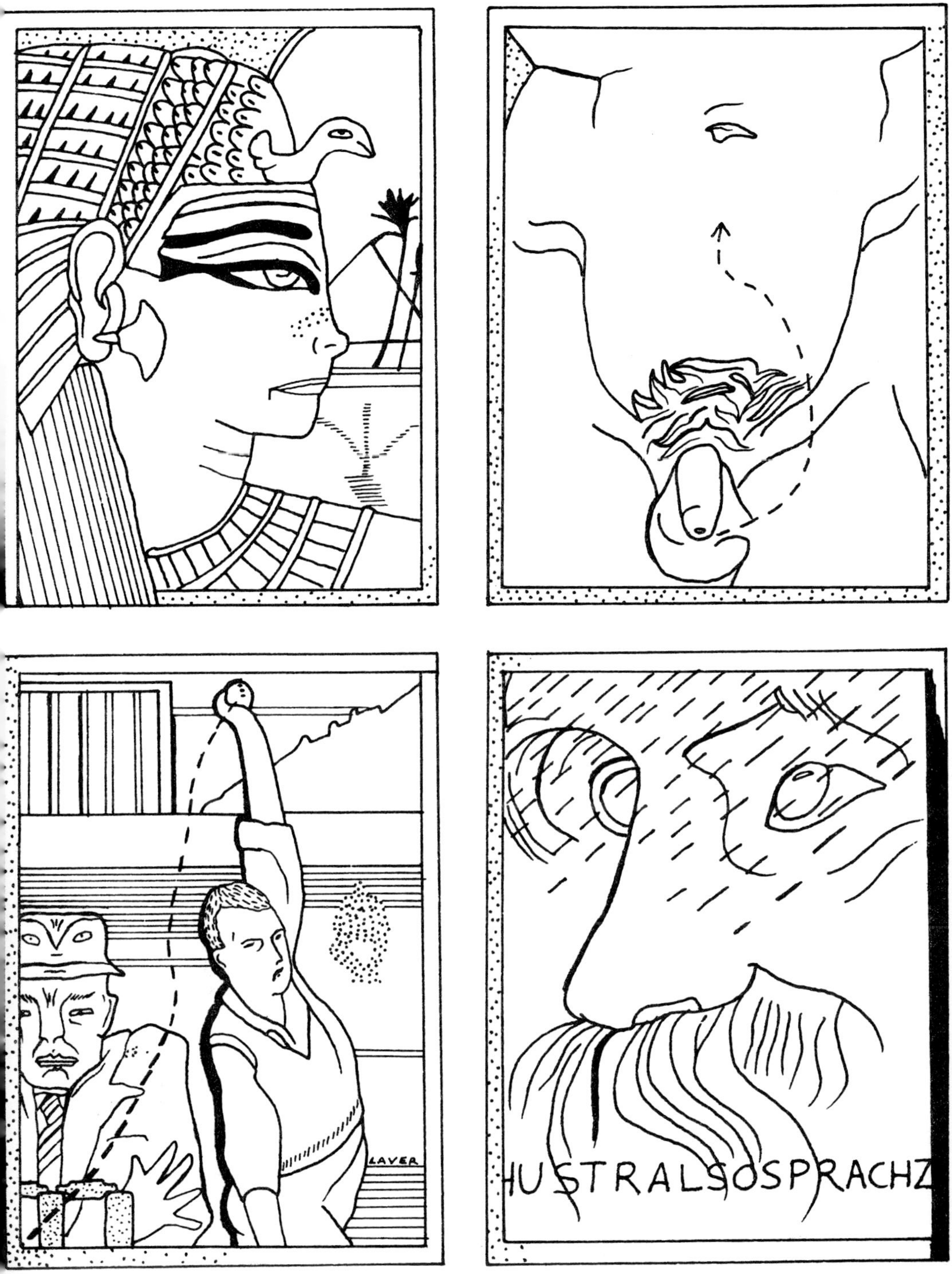
LAVER
HUSTRALSOSPRACHZ

OH, YOU CAN MISS IT

Turn left at Oaktree View;
Take care you do!
If not, then this
Will mean you'll surely miss
  The Plumbers' Institute.

It's been the plight of man
Since time began
To sigh and rue
That lapse at Oaktree View
  That loses him his route.

We learn in painful ways
Throughout our days
What Time can teach;
But shall we ever reach
  The Plumbers' Institute

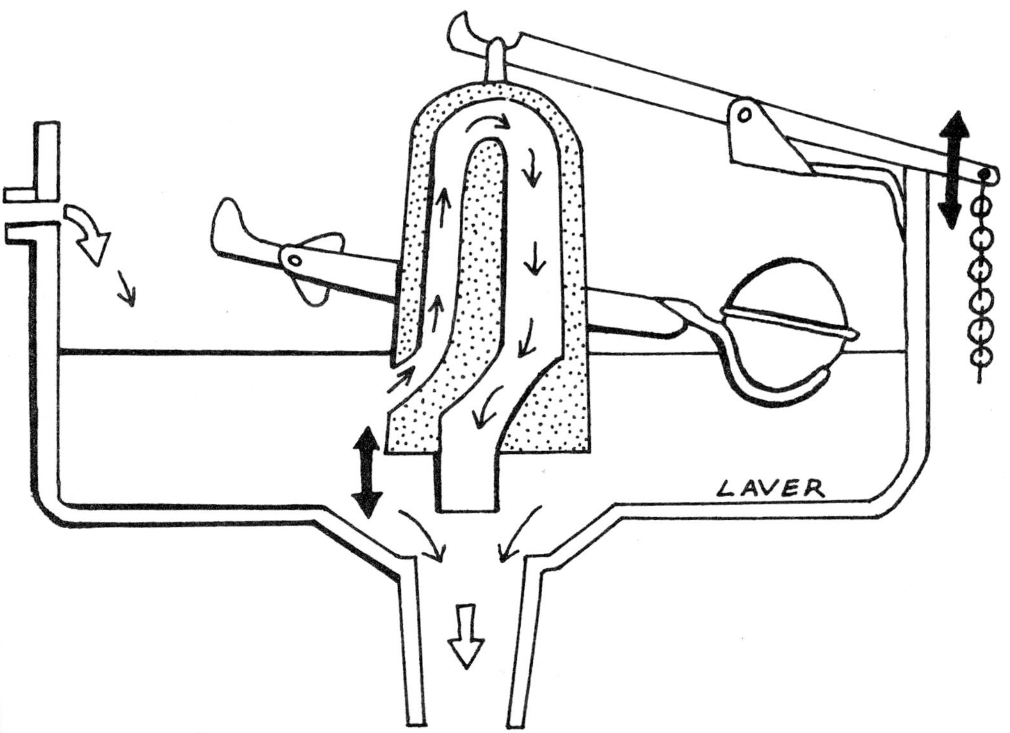
LAVER

AND WHERE WAS DAN McGREW ?

There were four of us chaps in that broken-down shack:
There was Big Buck and me, there was Sadie and Jack....
Four chaps did I say? – then just who was this Sadie?
No, she wasn't a chap, but she sure was no lady.

HOW DID THIS GET HERE?

I slobber when I eat; all right, I'm not quite nice.
That's not my only vice.
  I reckon women love a bloke
    That doesn't give a damn,
  And that's the way I am Drusilla,
    That's the way I am.

You're not the only lass: there's been a few before.
In nineteen-sixty-four,
  I felt this ginger lass's knees
    In Blackpool on a tram,
  For that's the way I am, Drusilla,
    That's the way I am.

You say you've met some men along the way,
  As tough as they can be.
You've never met a feller any day
  That's rotten mean, like me.

You'll take me as I am – you see, I just don't care!
And cross me if you dare,
  Because I'll up and pack my bags
    And go home to my mam.
  Oh, that's the way I am, Drusilla,
  That's the way I am.

LUST SONG

You swore you'd always worship me;
  You said we'd never part.
For all of three idyllic weeks,
  We lingered heart to heart.
Without a single backward glance,
  You then forsook my life.
Oh, why did you desert me thus
  Because I had a wife?

Your husband's eyes, you surely know,
  Have dwelt on Mrs Green,
Whose husband in his turn adores
  The wife of Roger Sheen;
And Roger loves my own dear wife:
  Of that there's little doubt.
God bless the swinging seventies
  For bringing this about.

I've found, I own, consoling arms,
  Although it's not the same,
With gorgeous Mrs Wilberforce
  And dishy Mrs Frame,
Whose husbands both, I understand,
  Find you all too sublime.
Why blame the swinging seventies?
  It's all as old as time.

FAT RUBY BLACK

Oh, that ancient downstairs flat amid the slums:
  That's the place where I first met fat Ruby Black;
That's where she and I were rather more than chums,
  With its cobbled lane and lavvy down the back.

They re-housed us, me and sweet fat Ruby Black,
  In these twenty-storey flats that reach the sky,
But her heart, I know, has never left that shack
  Where we lived in sin together, she and I.

Oh, fat Ruby Black! – the dreams aren't only yours
  And I'd love to take you back there on fine day,
For our nights were sweet behind those peeling doors –
  But they've pulled it down and built a motorway.

Oh, but love's a fickle thing that fades away,
  So when ours, fat Ruby Black, begins to cloy,
We can gaze down on that motorway and say:
  'Ah, now there's a lasting hymn to human joy!'

Red Ruby
services

LINES FORGOTTEN ON MARCH THE NINTH

When my knee is hurting and my chest is bad
And generally I'm rotten,
It conjures up those times we had;
Yes, I think of you –
Oo! –
The way you were last March the Seventh.

Oh, remembrance of that ghastly spring envenoms
The dream I dream twice nightly.
My God, you wore those awful denims!
And I can't forget
Yet
The way you were last March the Seventh.

It isn't just my chest and knee:
  I've suffered in more tender parts.
You seem to think your destiny
  Entitles you to break men's hearts.

When you've got your backache and the human race
Seems vilely represented
By one remembered ugly face,
I hope it'll be
Me
The way I was last March the Seventh.

HOW IT WASN'T

Beneath a clear blue sky we met in spring;
Our hearts together learned to sing.
  No sweeter song was sung,
  For we were very young,
You and I, you and I.

And through life's Summertime we stayed together,
Our heads held high against the weather.
  We never had much money,
  But always found life sunny,
You and I, you and I.

No matter what the season,
  Let the wind blow east or west,
There seems no rhyme or reason,
  But our love has stood the test.

When autumn's coming and the winter's cold,
As hand in hand we're growing old,
  We'll walk together still
  To go across the hill,
You and I, you and I.

MY REPULSIVE SWEETHEART

I hope you'll always be repulsive.
  Repulsive girls like you are few.
Oh,say you'll always be repulsive;
  I feel superior next to you.

You're good for my hysteria;
  You're keeping my neuroses new.
  I need someone that I can view
  With cold contempt, like you.

I hope you'll always be repulsive.
Don't do anything impulsive
  And suddenly grow pleasant, dear.
I hope you'll always be offensive;
Please keep my loathing quite extensive.
  And not for just the present, dear:
May you go on irritating,
May you feed my daily hating,
  And shine my phobias bright as any star.
Don't ever go away;
Say you'll always stay
  And always stay repulsive as you are.

Geoff Laws

TWA MILES FRAE HOGMANAY

Fiona McTavish, Fiona McTavish:
The favours she gave were exceedingly lavish.
  Oh, that lassie was most appetising.
Though you couldn't claim war
Could be laid at her door,
At her sensuous sway
As she walked down the brae,
  Every man in the clan would be rising.

Fiona McTavish, Fiona McTavish:
  How many braw lads did she manage to ravish
    In the fields of the oats and the barley?
Oh, she drained the physique
Of the strong and the weak:
Harry Lauder, Will Fyffe –
They were knock-kneed for life
    And Lord knows what she did to Prince Charlie.

AND NO REASON EITHER

When you were forty-five, my love,
  And I was eight-stone-two,
Your hair was ginger then I think,
  And I'd a stuffed-up nose.
          You called me king;
          I called you Ivy,
Although your name was Marguerite.
          Such bliss we knew!
          My socks were purple
And you were six feet six.

I never cease to think of you
  At least three times a year;
It may be four, but anyway,
  My thoughts come out in rhyme.

When I had influenze, love,
  Your bust was fifty-three.
It may be fifty-seven now:
  That's life, unless it's not.
          The days rolled by;
          So did your mother.
And Aston Villa won the cup.
          We said farewell;
          My heart was broken
And you had ginger hair. . .

DANDELION WHINE

About the dandelion – am I wrong? –
Not many singers sing their joyful song.
Amazingly prolific with its seeds,
The dandelion breeds, and breeds, and breeds.
Its crop ferments into a potent brew
Which knocks the Women's Institute askew.
Elizabethans called it piss-a-bed:
I don't know why; my mother never said.
It's brightly hued, but hardly wins on smell.
It spends its life just giving gardeners hell.
Not many sing about the dandelion:
I can't imagine why I'm even tryin'.

Notes On Artists

The artists featured are some of the regular contributors to IRON Magazine. For the first time they are assembled together in an IRON Press publication, providing their usual rich mix of styles. The deadpan drawings of Laver, the byzantine-like ornate cartoons of Hope, a dream world of high fantasy from Carole Senior, the ribald humour of Geoff Laws, the disturbing surrealism of John Spinks' contribution – all these and others. They give their widely different interpretations of Leonard Barras' comic verses, and provide an interesting dimension to the collection. Details of the artists are included alongside.

Pete Swan, Art Editor, IRON Press.

STEVEN HOPE was born on the banks of the river Tyne, went to Newcastle Art College, 1962–6. Afterwards got on a boat to Dublin where he has lived ever since. GEOFF LAWS was born in Blyth, spent some years in London, but is now back on Tyneside where he is the editorial artist for Thomson Newspapers. PETE LAVER married, interestingly. Two children. Phd. from Newcastle University on H.D. Thoreau's anarchism. At present working for the Wordsworth industry, at Dove Cottage, Grasmere. JOHN OLIVER was born 1956 in Hartlepool, now lives in Cullercoats. Works for Town Teacher on Newcastle's Quayside. Doesn't swim. MALCOLM MONTGOMERY was born on Tyneside in 1951, trained as a cabinet maker, then Art & Design Course at Newcastle Polytechnic. Lives at Walkergate, Tyneside. CAROLE SENIOR grew up in Sheffield, now lives on a bobbly hill near Abermule in Wales. Draws, writes, & chases chickens. JOHN SPINKS is from Tyneside, but has now moved to Northampton where he landed a good teaching job.

IRON Press is a non-commercial outfit struggling to bring new work into print. We also publish IRON, a quarterly literary magazine which since 1973 has featured the work of more than 400 authors, world-wide. The press Drama Series makes available the leading contemporary plays from the North-East. Two more of our publications are listed overleaf and can be ordered direct by post (plus 12p p & p). Our address is at the front of this book if you'd like to know more.

IRON
PRESS